Anthony Brayn

Master keys on how to invest

Contents

1.

2.

    1.

      2.

        3.

3.

    1.

      2.

        3.

4.

    1.

      2.

        3.

5.

    1.

      2.

    3.

6.
   1.
      2.
         3.
7.
   1.
   2.
   3.
   4.
   5.
   6.
   7.
   8.
   9.

Preface

While money doesn't grow on trees, it can grow when you save and invest wisely.

Knowing how to secure your financial well-being is one of the most important things you'll ever need in life. You don't have to be a genius to do it. You just need to know a few basics, form a plan, and be ready to stick to it. No matter how much or little money you have, the important thing is to educate yourself about your opportunities. In this brochure, we'll cover the basics on saving and investing.

At the SEC, we enforce the laws that determine how investments are offered and sold to you. These laws protect in- vectors, but you need to do your part, too. Part of this brochure tells you how to check out investments and the people that sell them so you do not fall victim to fraud or costly mistakes.

No one can guarantee that you'll make money from investments you make. But if you get the facts about sav- ing and investing and follow through with an intelligent plan, you should be able to gain financial security over the years and enjoy the benefits of managing your money.

Please feel free to contact us with any of your ques- tions or concerns about investing. It always pays to learn before you invest. And congratulations on taking your first step on the road to financial security!

Don't Wait to Get Started

YOU CAN DO IT!

IT'S EASIERTHANYOUTHINK.

No one is born knowing how to save or to invest. Every successful investor starts with the basics—the information in this brochure.

A few people may stumble into financial security—a wealthy relative may die, or a business may take off. But for most peo- ple, the only way to attain financial security is to save and in- vest over a long period of time.

Time after time, people of even modest means who begin the journey reach financial security and all that it promises: buying a home, educational opportunities for their children, and a comfortable retirement. If they can do it, so can you!

1

INVESTMENT

•What Exactly Is A Financial Investment Or Monetary ventures

•What precisely is financial investment

Meaning of Financial investment Or monetary ventures

Have you heard somebody discussing stocks, securities, or shared reserves and were somewhat befuddled? Does the notice of ventures or monetary points appear to be overpowering? Seeing some essential data about monetary speculations can be an extraordinary initial phase in figuring out how to contribute, knowing your way to retirement, or expanding the pace of return on your cash. It is human instinct to anticipate stormy days. An individual should plan and save to the side some measure of cash for any undeniable situation which could emerge in days to come.Future is questionable and one should put astutely to stay away from monetary emergency in any place of time.

Allow us first to comprehend what is Investment ?

Investment is only products or wares bought today to be utilized in future or at the hours of emergency. An individual should design his future well to guarantee joy for himself as well as his close relatives. Consuming everything today and saving nothing for what's in store is absurd. Not regular is a walk in the park, no one can tell what your future has coming up for you.

What is Monetary Venture Or Financial Investment ?

Monetary venture alludes or financial investment to setting to the side a decent measure of cash and expecting some sort of gain out of it inside a specified time period.

One more significance for monetary venture is a resource that you put cash into with the expectation that it will develop or appreciate into a bigger amount of cash. The thought is that you can later sell it at a greater cost or bring in cash on it while you own it. You might be hoping to develop something over the course of the following year, for example, putting something aside for a vehicle, or over the course of the following 30 years, like putting something aside for retirement.

How you contribute these dollars can be altogether different. How long you have on your side is in many cases something critical to consider while making a monetary speculation. The additional time you have, the more gamble you can normally take. The more gamble you take, the more potential for getting more cash! It is vital to take note of that there is likewise a monetary meaning of monetary speculations that arrangements with how organizations put resources into items, hardware, plants, representatives, and inventories. This example will zero in on the money meaning of monetary venture. We should take a gander at a couple of key terms worth knowing with regards to monetary speculations.

Appreciation is the sum a venture fills in esteem. For instance, you purchase a portion of stock for $10, and after a year it is valued at $15; the stock has appreciated $5.

Profits are generally cash installments that are paid out on monetary ventures in view of the achievement and profit of an organization. For instance, you put resources into Microsoft stock, and it might deliver you a profit of $5 an offer. In the event that you claimed 500 offers you would get compensated 500 * $5 which is $2,500!

Premium is the charge a bank, foundation, or government pays you for crediting them cash through the acquisition of a Disc or bond. You can likewise procure limited quantities of premium on a checking or bank account. For instance, you might have $10,000 in government reserve funds securities that pays 5% interest every year; that amounts to $500 per year!

•Financial and Economic Meaning of Investment

Investment is the work of assets determined to get return on it. Overall terms, speculation implies the utilization of cash in the desire for getting more cash. In finance, speculation implies the acquisition of a monetary item or other thing of significant worth with an assumption for great future returns. Venture of hard brought in cash is a pivotal action of each and every person. Investment is the responsibility of assets which have been saved from current utilization with the expectation that a few advantages will be gotten in future. In this way, it is a prize for sitting tight for cash. Reserve funds of individuals are put resources into resources relying upon their gamble and bring requests back. Speculation alludes to the idea of conceded utilization, which includes buying a resource, giving a credit or keeping supports in a ledger fully intent on producing future returns. Different venture choices are accessible, offering contrasting gamble reward trade offs. A comprehension of the center ideas and a careful investigation of the choices can assist a financial backer with making a portfolio that expands returns while limiting gamble openness.

There are Two ideas of Venture:

1) Economic Investment or Financial Speculation: The idea of monetary venture implies expansion to the capital supply of the general public. The capital load of the general public is the merchandise which are utilized in the development of different products. The term venture suggests the arrangement of new and useful capital as new development and makers sturdy instrument like plant and apparatus. Inventories and human resources are likewise remembered for this idea. Subsequently, a venture, in monetary terms, implies an expansion in building, gear, and stock.

2) Financial investment or Monetary Venture: This is a distribution of financial assets to resources that are supposed to yield some increase or return over a given time frame. It implies a trade of monetary cases like offers and bonds, land, and so on. Monetary speculation includes contrasts composed on bits of paper like offers and debentures. Individuals put their assets in shares, debentures, fixed stores, public saving testaments, disaster protection arrangements, opportune asset and so forth in their view speculation is a responsibility of assets to determine future pay as interest, profits, lease, charges, annuity benefits and the enthusiasm for the worth of their chief capital. In crude economies most ventures are of the genuine assortment though in a cutting edge economy much speculation is of the monetary assortment.

The monetary and monetary ideas of venture are connected with one another in light of the fact that speculation is a piece of the reserve funds of people which stream into the capital market either straightforwardly or through foundations. In this manner, venture choices and monetary choices associate with one another. Monetary choices are fundamentally worried about the wellsprings of cash where as venture choices are generally worried about utilizes or planning of cash.

So from above we know the term speculation. The savers become the financial backers in the accompanying term and put resources into novel resources:

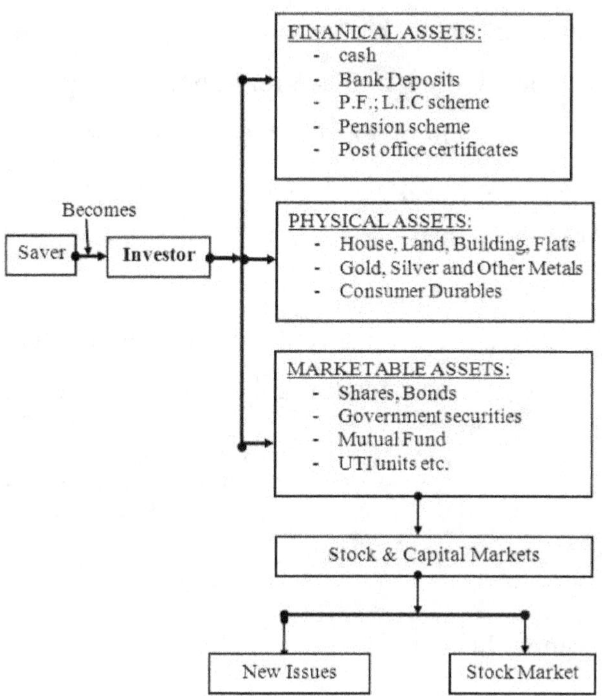

•Types of Investment or ventures

Savvy financial backers know not to tie up their resources in one place aimlessly. All things being equal, they come out as comfortable with one or two kinds of ventures and utilize their insight into each to bring in cash in various ways.

With regards to effective financial planning, there are a ton of containers to browse. In any case, it's critical to see every one of your choices before you really put away your cash and begin to construct your portfolio.

Each sort of speculation has its potential gain and drawback. The best sorts of speculations to make rely upon your gamble resistance, level of comprehension of specific business sectors, course of events to keep away from capital gains, and purposes behind putting resources into the primary spot.

Among the various kinds of speculations out there, there are likely a not many that will function admirably for you so we should get into it.

Section Guide

Cash and commodities
    Bonds and Securities
    Investment Funds
    The Stock Market
    Retirement Plans
    Real Estate
    Non-Ventures to Keep away from
    What are the Best Sorts of Investment?

•Cash and commodities or money and wares

Money and wares are regularly viewed as generally safe kinds of speculations, so on the off chance that you're new to financial planning or are awkwardly with any gamble, one of these choices could be a decent spot to begin. Remember that okay ventures additionally will quite often have low returns.

1. Gold

Indeed, you can put resources into gold and different products like silver or unrefined petroleum. Truth be told, the act of putting resources into gold goes way back, however that doesn't be guaranteed to mean it's an extraordinary venture. Gold is a product, so its cost depends on shortage and dread, which can be influenced by political activities or ecological changes.

On the off chance that you are putting resources into gold, know that your "channel" (insurance against a cost drop), depends on outside factors - so the cost can vary a ton, and rapidly. The value will in general go up when shortage and dread are plentiful and down when gold is broadly free.

In the event that you think the world will be a more unfortunate spot from now on, then, at that point, gold could be a wise speculation for you.

Key Action item:

What to recall is that wagering on products, for example, gold is typically only that — wagering. It's not Rule #1 Contributing except if you Realize that shortage will provoke an interest for gold and drive up the cost.

2. Bank Products and CD's

Bank products are investment types presented by banks that incorporate investment accounts and currency market accounts. Currency market accounts are like bank accounts, yet normally procure higher loan fees as a trade-off for higher equilibrium prerequisites.

A Cd, or declaration of store, is one more sort of bank item. At the point when you buy a Cd you consent to credit the bank a measure of cash for an assigned measure of time to procure a higher measure of revenue on it than you would in a run of the mill bank account.

Compact discs are an incredibly okay speculation - however with generally safe, comes low award. Most banks offer Compact discs at an arrival of under 2% each year, which isn't sufficiently even to stay aware of expansion.

Key Action item:

Try not to throw away your energy on CDs. While they can be a protected spot to set aside your cash and get somewhat more premium than you would in a bank account, they are certainly not an extraordinary spot to develop your cash.

3. Cryptocurrency

Cryptocurrency forms of money are one of the more current sorts of speculation. They are unregulated computerized monetary standards traded on digital money sites.

Digital currencies, like Bitcoin or Doge coin, have acquired a great deal of revenue lately as a speculation vehicle because of their fast and emotional development. In any case, they stay a staggeringly hazardous speculation due to the numerous obscure elements related with them.

There is the chance of unofficial law and the likelihood that digital money won't ever consider boundless acknowledgment to be a type of installment. Cryptocurrency money at present has no characteristic worth and it could vanish as fast as it appeared.

The most effective method to Put resources into Bitcoin

Similarly that you can trade US Dollars for some other money, for example, Yens or Euros, you can likewise trade your US Dollars for digital currencies.

However digital forms of money aren't actually essential for the Forex market, the mechanics of putting resources into cryptocurrency forms of money is basically the same. The desire for some digital money financial backers is that the worth of those digital forms of money goes facing the dollar, and they are moderately easy to purchase on the web.

Somebody who put resources into Bitcoin in 2013 and sold it today would positively create a few mind boggling gains. The issue is that it's absolutely impossible to time the digital currency market. Bitcoin and other digital currencies could proceed to emphatically increment in cost, or they could drop to nothing.

Key Focal point:

Remove my recommendation and remain. As of now, nobody knows without a doubt what's on the horizon for digital currencies, so putting resources into digital forms of money is minimal more than hypothesis. We don't put resources into things we don't comprehend in light of the fact that that is simply betting.

Bonds and Securities(protection)

Bonds and securities are different sorts of generally safe ventures. Bonds can be bought from the US government, state and regional authorities, or from individual organizations.

Contract upheld securities are a sort of bond that is regularly given by an organization of the U.S. government, however can likewise be given by a confidential firm.

4. U.S. Savings Bonds and Corporate Bonds

At the point when you buy any sort of security, you are crediting cash to the substance you buy it from for a foreordained measure of time and premium.

Bonds are viewed as protected and generally safe in light of the fact that the possibly opportunity of not getting your cash back is on the off chance that the guarantor defaults. U.S. saving securities are securities supported by the U.S. government, which makes them nearly sans risk.

Legislatures issue Bonds to fund-raise for undertakings and tasks, and the equivalent is valid for organizations who issue Bonds.

Corporate Bonds are somewhat more hazardous than government securities since there's more gamble of an enterprise defaulting on the credit. Dissimilar to when you put resources into an organization by buying its stock, buying a corporate Bonds doesn't give you any possession in that organization.

A significant note to recall is that a bonds may just net you a 3% profit from your cash over numerous years. This implies that when you remove your cash from the bonds, you'll really have less purchasing power than when you put it in light of the fact that the pace of development didn't actually stay aware of the pace of expansion.

Key Focal point:

There isn't anything "protected" about hitting bottom financially in retirement on the grounds that your paces of return couldn't stay aware of expansion while you were attempting to develop and safeguard your cash. It's not worth the effort to place your cash in bonds.

5. Mortgage Backed securities

At the point when you buy a Mortgage Backed securities , you are by and by loaning cash to a bank or government establishment, however your credit is supported by a pool of home and other land contracts.

Like shared reserves, Index funds are one of the kinds of corporate stocks that enhances your investment across various stocks. The distinction between Index funds and Mutual funds is that Index funds are patently made due, not straightforwardly supervised by a cash supervisor.

Since index funds or file reserves are patently made due, there are less charges included, and that implies you have the potential for somewhat better yields than with a shared asset. In any case, your profits will be founded altogether on how well the list your asset is following does.

Considering that most significant index are utilized to follow the general development of the market, they perform probably as well as the general market does in the extremely long haul. All in all, they will generally yield a typical return of around 7% each year.

While this isn't quite as high as the profits you can accomplish through effectively picking individual organizations with the right examination, a good return is impressively higher than the loan costs of an investment account or the return paces of bonds.

At the point when you put resources into a file, you're basically wagering your cash on the eventual fate of America. Assuming you're certain the American economy will continue developing, you're presumably going to come out alright.

The issue here is that assuming that you put your cash into a file, and we go into a downturn, the market could be down for a lot of time. That implies your portfolio will likewise be down, and assuming you're excessively near retirement to trust that things will swing back the alternate way, you could be in a difficult situation.

That is one more in addition to of putting resources into individual organizations. The truly extraordinary ones will generally perform, even in the midst of downturn.

Key Focus point:

If you would rather not accomplish the work (and receive the benefits) of figuring out how to put resources into individual organizations, a list store is a decent "put your cash in and just drop it" choice that will regularly produce improved results than a common asset.

<u>**Investment Funds**</u>

Investment funds are made up of a pool of money collected from multiple investors that are then invested into many different things including, stocks, bonds, and other assets. The collection of investments typically tracks a market index.

6. Mutual Funds

A mutual fund is a type of investment fund operated by a money manager who invests your money for you, and attempts to get good returns.

Mutual funds are typically made up of a combination of stocks and bonds, however, they carry less risk because your money is diversified across many stocks and bonds. You'll only reap rewards from stock dividends and bond interest, or if you sell when the value of the fund goes up with the market.

The average individual will need more than $3 million to be financially independent in retirement in twenty years and, frankly, mutual funds won't get you there.

When it comes to value, remember that mutual funds are built and managed by so-called "financial experts" who have a hard time beating the market, especially when you factor in the fees they're charging you to manage your money in the first place.

Rule #1 Investors expect a minimum annual compounded rate of return of 15% a year or more. If we can get that, we don't care what the market did because we're going to retire rich anyway.

Key Takeaway:

You'll have a much easier time (and more fun!) learning how to invest your own money rather than relying on some mutual fund manager who can't beat the market.

7. Index Funds

Similar to mutual funds, index funds are one of the types of stock investments that diversifies your investment across multiple stocks. The difference between index funds and mutual funds is that index funds are passively managed, not directly overseen by a money manager.

Because index funds are passively managed, there are less fees involved, which means you have the potential for slightly higher returns than with a mutual fund. However, your returns will be based entirely on how well the index your fund is tracking does.

Given that most major indexes are used to track the overall movement of the market, they perform about as well as the overall market does in the very long term. In other words, they tend to yield an average return of about 7% per year.

While this isn't as high as the returns you can achieve through successfully picking individual companies with the right research, it IS a respectable return that is considerably higher than the interest rates of a savings account or the return rates of bonds.

When you invest in an index, you're essentially betting your money on the future of America. If you're confident the American economy will keep growing, you're probably going to come out OK.

The problem here is that if you put your money into an index, and we go into a recession, the market could be down for a significant amount of time. That means your portfolio will also be down, and if you're too close to retirement to wait for things to swing back the other way, you could be in trouble.

That's another plus of investing in individual companies. The really great ones tend to perform, even in times of recession.

Key Takeaway:

If you don't want to do the work (and reap the rewards) of learning to invest in individual companies, an index fund is a good "put your money in and forget about it" option that will typically generate better results than a mutual fund.

8. Exchange Traded Funds Or Trade Exchanged Assets

Trade Exchanged Assets, or ETFs as they're usually called, are like record supports in that they track a famous file and mirror its presentation. Dissimilar to record reserves, however, ETFs are traded on the securities exchange.

Since ETFs are exchanged on the securities exchange, you have more command over what cost you buy them at and will pay less charges. Your prize is totally reliant upon how well or how inadequately the record you put resources into performs.

You can limit your gamble by putting resources into an ETF that tracks an expansive file, like the S&P 500.

Essentially placing your cash in a trade exchanged reserve like the S&P 500 (SPY), an assortment of the 500 greatest organizations on the lookout, permits you to benefit from the market's development without paying expenses to an asset chief.

Key Important point:

Beside putting resources into individual organizations, an ETF is most likely the most ideal choice amateur financial backers have accessible.

<u>The Stock market or financial exchange</u>

There are various ways of putting resources into the stock Market . As I referenced above, you could put resources into a securities exchange file, or you could contribute with investment opportunities, or — and this one's my #1 — you could put resources into individual stocks.

9. Individual Stocks

Stocks are "shares" of proprietorship in a specific organization. At the point when you buy a singular organization's stock, you become a halfway proprietor of that organization. That implies when the organization brings in cash, you do as well, and when the organization fills in esteem, the worth of your stock develops also.

At the point when the cost of an organization's stock goes up, the worth of the proprietor's interest in that organization goes up. The proprietor can then decide to sell the stock for a benefit. Be that as it may, when the cost of an organization's stock goes down, the worth of the proprietor's speculation goes down.

Stock proprietors can likewise get rewards by means of profits in the event that the organization decides to convey profit to their investors.

It is feasible to accomplish a lot higher than normal returns by putting resources into hand-chose individual organizations you've investigated. You can limit your gamble by putting resources into just brilliant organizations at costs that ensure a major return. That is the Standard #1 way.

Key Focus point:

Among the numerous things to put resources into, stocks are my undisputed top choice and by a long shot the most fulfilling. The best financial backers put resources into stocks since you can improve returns than with some other venture type. Warren Buffet turned into an effective financial backer by purchasing portions of stocks, and you can as well.

10. Stock Options Or Investment opportunities

At the point when you buy a choice in an organization, you are wagering that the cost of that organization's stock will go up or down. Buying a choice permits you to trade portions of that organization at a set cost inside a set time period, without really possessing the stock.

Investment opportunities are unbelievably hazardous. Similarly as with most high-risk sorts of ventures, there is potential for exceptional yields. Tragically , there is additionally the potential for extraordinary misfortune - particularly in the event that you don't have the foggiest idea what you're doing

Put Choices Or Call option

With a call option, you're consenting to SELL a stock when it gets to a specific cost at a particular time. With a CALL OPTION , you're consenting to Purchase a stock at a specific cost at a particular time.

PUT choices can be considered like insurance contracts. You get them at a set cost, over a specific time frame and sell the stock no matter what the cost. Financial backers by and large purchase PUTS when they are worried that the market will fall. This is on the grounds that a PUT gives you the option to sell a stock at a proper cost, and it will normally increment in esteem if the cost of the basic stock begins to drop.

Call Choices

CALL choices have a market value, alluded to as a premium. You pay the premium of the call choice to tie down the agreement to purchase the basic stock.

Putting resources into CALL choices is an incredible method for producing income and lessen premise on organizations we currently own.

Key Focal point:

Notwithstanding stocks, choices are a decent decision in the event that you are searching for exceptional yield kinds of ventures. Nonetheless, I don't suggest putting resources into choices for fledglings.

•<u>Retirement Plans</u>

There are two significant sorts of retirement accounts: a 401K and an IRA. The two records are comprised of money you set to the side and afterward put resources into different ways.

The gamble and compensation of retirement accounts are totally reliant upon what they are put resources into, which can change significantly. Notwithstanding these retirement accounts, annuities are another venture type that you might need to consider as a feature of your retirement

Sorts of Speculations

What Will Get You the Most Cash-flow?

Shrewd financial backers know not to tie up their assets in one place aimlessly. All things considered, they come out as comfortable with maybe one or two sorts of ventures and utilize their insight into each to bring in cash in various ways.

With regards to financial planning, there are a ton of bushels to browse. However, it's critical to see every one of your choices before you really put away your cash and begin to fabricate your portfolio.

11. 401k

A 401k is a retirement account presented by your boss. The large advantage of this retirement choice is that your boss might offer a "match", and that implies they will match how much cash you put into your record - up to a specific rate.

The Enormous Issue with 401ks

All of the cash put resources into a 401(k) winds up in shared reserves. The issue is that these shared assets quite often neglect to beat the market normal.

All in all, just placing your cash into a file, for example, the S&P 500 and leaving it there with zero administration would in any case net you a bigger number of profits than you are probably going to see when you put resources into a 401(k).

The motivation behind why shared reserves neglect to beat the market indeed returns to the way that the supervisors of these assets charge an impressive expense for their administrations. When this charge is deducted, any profits that the director had the option to yield past the general market's exhibition are immediately reduced.

Keep in mind, expanding your speculation portfolio doesn't innately imply that you are bringing down your true capacity for risk.

Key Important point:

401ks are not something that ought to be stayed away from in all circumstances. A business match that pairs your speculation is quite often worth the effort. Nonetheless, they ought not be depended on as your only method for speculation.

Adhere to the business match. Putting anything else than that in a 401k is only a squandered an open door.

12. IRA

An IRA is a singular retirement account you can set up for yourself. As far as IRAs, there are customary IRAs (charge conceded) and Roth IRAs (is tax-exempt).

Indeed, you read that accurately. A Roth IRA is tax-exempt!

The cash you put resources into a Roth IRA is burdened before it is contributed, so when you take it out during retirement you're not burdened on the pay from your speculations.

With both an IRA and a Roth IRA, you have more command over where you put away your cash than you do with a 401K. You can decide to put the cash in these records in individual stocks, securities, ETFs, and shared reserves.

The more control you have over your ventures and the more broadened they are, the less gamble you face.

Key Action item:

Regardless of what your identity is or where you work, a Roth IRA is one of the most outstanding things to put resources into on the grounds that you can have all out command over what it is put resources into and your cash develops tax-exempt! Maximize it and contribute it the Standard #1 way.

13. Annuities

Annuities are an agreement between a financial backer and an insurance agency where the financial backer pays a singular amount in return for occasional installments made by the guarantor. They are regularly used to enhance pay and lock down a consistent regularly scheduled installment during retirement.

There's no genuine gamble to annuities, however there's no genuine opportunity of get back by the same token. They are just a method for saving pay for retirement, not guarantee development.

Key Focal point:

While annuities might be useful for certain retired folks, they are not an ideal speculation choice for novice financial backers who are looking to develop their cash as a matter of fact.

<u>**Real Estate**</u>

There are different ways of putting resources into real estate from purchasing homes, condos, and business structures to flipping houses, or in any event, claiming ranches and trailer parks. The primary disadvantage for most starting financial backers is that the cost of passage is high.

14. Property

Property is much of the time a costly venture, which can undoubtedly swarm out little financial backers with less capital.

Notwithstanding, swarm financed land speculation valuable open doors are starting to spring up, giving new kinds of ventures to the people who need to put resources into land however don't have all the money.

The hardest part about putting resources into land is finding a property that you can buy with an edge of security. In the event that you can do that, you can make a few nice returns putting resources into property.

You can bring in cash by purchasing the property at a beneath market rate and selling it at the maximum, as well as by leasing or renting the property to occupants.

The different kinds of property ventures can be generally great, the length of you treat them equivalent to some other Rule #1 speculation. This implies the property ought to have importance to you, have a canal, great administration, and be bought with an edge of security.

Key Focal point:

While it's feasible to find an extraordinary arrangement on land, it very well may be more straightforward to put resources into the securities exchange, make similar returns or better, and not need to manage having a lot of investment properties to deal with.

15. Real Estate Investments Trust

Real estate investment trust, or REIT, is like a mutual fund in that it takes the assets of numerous financial backers and puts them in an assortment of pay producing land properties.

In addition, REITs can be traded like stocks on the financial exchange so they can be less expensive and more straightforward to put resources into than property.

Without purchasing, make due, or finance any properties yourself, putting resources into a REIT diminishes the hindrances of passage normal to property land venture.

Key Focal point:

You needn't bother with truckload of cash and you don't have to stress over keeping up with the properties. While you won't get as much cash-flow from property appreciation, you can get a consistent pay   from   REITs.

2

IMPORTANCE OF INVESTMENT

•The Importance of Investment

Importance of investment which also know as Significance of speculation

Today we will discuss putting away your cash which is the best way to acquire independence from the rat race in the long haul. Contributing is the most ideal way to bring in your cash bring in additional cash for yourself and secure your future simultaneously.

We earnestly trust that you have previously begun money management. In the event that not, then, at that point, you should begin today to get the accompanying convincing advantages.

1. It is an incredible wellspring of automated revenue

One thing that the continuous COVID emergency has shown us is that we can't exclusively depend on your customary pay. In the event that we can't procure our standard pay for reasons unknown, we can land up in tremendous difficulties.

To relieve this gamble, you should have a second line of pay which will assist you with supporting yourself in the midst of such emergency. This can be your interests in Fixed stores, values, Common Assets, properties, and different resources. These speculations will keep on acquiring returns for you in any event, when your standard pay pauses and empower you to easily hold over the circumstance.

2. Brings monetary Freedom

Could it be said that you fear becoming subject to others after retirement for your financial requirements? You can definitely relax. You can get independence from the rat race in your advanced age by money management routinely to make a retirement Corpus. The recurring, automated revenue you will acquire from this corpus will empower you to deal with your month to month expenses and different requirements easily after retirement.

3. It allows you to follow your enthusiasm

Do you fantasy about resigning right on time to seek after an energy that you have? In the event that indeed, your ventures are the way to accomplishing your fantasy. Your technique ought to be to put and gather abundance in an arranged manner in your initial years and when you collect a sizable riches, resign early.

The recurring, automated revenue you procure from those speculations will assist you with meeting your costs from there on while you are occupied in effectively seeking after your enthusiasm.

4. Assists with beating expansion

Expansion is an unavoidable truth which not even one of us can keep away from. It diminishes the buying influence of cash we have and makes us more unfortunate as time elapses by. Except if you do whatever it takes to resolve this issue, you can be in some hot water.

The most ideal way to battle the adverse consequence of expansion is to put the cash that you have in your grasp today. Contributing consistently will empower you to beat expansion and your buying power won't go down.

5. Get tax cuts

Did you had any idea about that your speculations can get you tax reductions as well? Different speculation items like PPF, ELSS, Assessment Saving Securities and long haul fixed stores offer tax cuts under area 80C of the Annual Expense Act 1961. Put resources into them shrewdly to diminish your taxation rate.

You want to begin putting consistently in a trained manner to get the advantages I have discussed. Allow your cash to transform into a sizable abundance over the long haul and gain the independence from the rat race that you long for.

Importance of financial investment

In the event that you're simply beginning, starting a speculation program might be something that hasn't been on your radar. You might be more worried about how to pay for things like food and fuel. In any case, on the off chance that you can figure out even a modest quantity of cash for speculation purposes, you'll be en route to making a lot rosier monetary picture in the years to come.

TL;DR (Excessively Lengthy; Didn't Peruse)

Having monetary speculations or Financial investment is significant in light of the fact that your investment (ventures) can assist you with beating expansion, save for retirement, set your cash to work and act as extra monetary assets.

Beating The Expansion Rate

As well as making for awkward dozing, stuffing your cash under a sleeping cushion does close to nothing to moderate the effect of expansion over the long haul. Placing your cash in an ordinary bank account won't help much either in view of the regularly minute financing costs. While putting your cash in venture vehicles, like stocks and common assets, presents a component of hazard, you have a greatly improved possibility of dominating the expansion rate all through a time of years.

Putting something aside For Retirement

Contingent exclusively upon Federal retirement aide benefits as your wellspring of retirement pay most likely won't slice it except if you intend to stay alive on a tight eating routine of rice and water. Except if your organization offers a sizable benefits plan, you will most likely need to begin a venture program as soon as conceivable to guarantee an agreeable retirement. IRAs offer a simple method for financial planning for retirement and furthermore give specific tax breaks. On the off chance that your boss offers a 401(k) plan, you can profit from the matching subsidizes that many organizations will store in your record for your sake.

Giving Your Cash Something to do

On the off chance that you have some work, you're without a doubt acquainted with the idea of working for your cash. Contributing permits you to switch things around by bringing in your cash work for you. Through the wizardry of self multiplying dividends, for instance, your gathered revenue really brings in extra cash easily. Subsequently, your unique speculation can duplicate incredibly over the long run. For instance, assuming you contributed $1,000 at a financing cost of 7% accumulated every year, your speculation would develop to $7,612.26 following 30 years.

Having More Monetary Assets

A few speculations can satisfy more than one monetary reason and act as an important asset. For example, when you buy a home, it might see the value in worth and return an attractive benefit when you sell it. Furthermore, as you make your month to month contract installments you develop value, which is how much your proprietorship stake in the property. You can get against your gathered value by taking out a home value credit or home value credit extension to help you more quick monetary requirements.

Before we go over the particulars of what you ought to consider putting resources into, be it stocks, bonds, or your cousin Brian's yakalo ranch — we should initially go over the fundamentals of how one contributes.

Contributing happens when toward the month's end, after the bills are paid, you have a couple of dollars left over to put towards your future. No putting away occurs without taking care of cash. How are you expected to track down those tricky additional dollars to save? This is the way.

Keep away from way of life creep

Probably, you'll acquire more in your thirties than you did in your twenties, and, surprisingly, more than that in your forties. The way to saving is to put forth a valiant effort to stay away from what's classified "way of life creep". In the event that you haven't known about this previously, let us make sense of.

Way of life creep actually intends that as you get more cash-flow, what once seemed like extravagances become necessities. Entire cooked pigeon and shellfish concassé might be eminent and everything except in light of the fact that you have the $626 in your financial records to cover the tasting menu at Fellow Savoy doesn't mean you ought to. All things considered, you ought to give your all to experience the same way you've generally lived. Then, at that point, set aside the additional cash you're making from your raises instead of increment your spending. Skirt the pigeon, get yourself a croquet monsieur, and contribute the 600 bucks you saved!

Begin Investing — even a little at a time

Whenever you have reserve funds, you'll totally need to contribute. Expansion will quite often outperform the loan cost that you'll have the option to get on an investment account. You'll be successfully be setting aside and losing cash simultaneously. For this reason you ought to begin effective money management straightaway.

Contributing isn't only for the Warren Smorgasbord's of the world. In the event that you are tracking down it extreme to take care of some putting away cash every month, have a go at utilizing a loose coinage application. These administrations gather together your buys, permitting you to put away modest quantities of cash that you'd barely miss. For instance, on the off chance that you burned through $3.39 on an espresso, $0.61 would be contributed.

Putting away limited quantities of cash is an extraordinary propensity to get into and your cash will accumulate over the long haul. Assuming you're searching for additional simple methods for putting away with minimal expenditure, they are right here.

Understand what you're effective money management for

How you contribute relies upon what precisely you're money management for. You may be putting away cash to assist your 14 year old with her forthcoming college educational cost. You should put away cash to live off when you resign in 30 years or something like that. The time skylines on every one of these ventures are altogether different. Since you'll require admittance to some of them sooner than others. Those with more limited skylines ought to contribute all the more safely. Those putting away cash they don't require for quite a while can pick more dangerous speculations.

Comprehend the gamble you are taking

Prior to choosing where to contribute, you'll have to initially evaluate your own gamble resistance. This is an extravagant approach to saying the amount of your venture you can truly bear to lose. On the off chance that you want cash for the following month's lease, you have an extremely generally safe resistance. On the off chance that your life wouldn't be substantially impacted in any capacity, if as opposed to putting away cash, you put a match to it, your gamble resistance is through the rooftop. Risk resistance is frequently directed by your purported "time skyline". This might seem like something you'd hear on the scaffold of the Star ship Venture, yet all things being equal, simply a term implies the time frame you'll hold a specific speculation.

Investment accounts are regularly viewed as okay. They are fitting for holding your secret stash, stormy day cash, or this month lease. Contributing is substantially more fit to cash you don't require for the time being, for instance your retirement reserve funds, or an asset for your kid's college degree.

Enhance your speculations or diversify your investment.

As opposed to focus in on some stock you think will perform well, enhance your speculations. In doing this, in the event that one piece of your speculation doesn't do well you haven't lost everything. Michael Allen, a Portfolio Chief at Wealth simple makes sense of that broadening your portfolio implies putting resources into various topographies, ventures, and resource classes (stocks, bonds, land and so on).

It makes sense of that vacillations aren't really the greatest gamble for financial backers in it for the long stretch. A possibly greater gamble is the means by which you respond to the variances. Numerous financial backers find it challenging to adhere to their effective money management plan — especially during market developments. An expanded portfolio that is inclined to less market developments can prove to be handy to assist with dealing with your feelings.

Assuming this portfolio expansion talk seems as though difficult work — that is on the grounds that it is. Robotized contributing is a decent option for somebody who needs to enhance their portfolio however doesn't have any desire to go to the work of purchasing different resources like stocks, bonds and land without anyone else.

Contribute as long as possible

On the off chance that you would be able, contribute as long as possible. Many examinations show that financial backers who clutch stocks for over 10 years will be compensated with more significant yields that offset transient dangers. Saying this doesn't imply that this pattern will proceed, or that hazard is at any point completely disposed of. Risk never vanishes, yet you could say it progresses with age.

On the off chance that you can take care of cash for quite a while period, then, at that point, you can stand to have ventures that are normally more powerless to rising and falling. Your portfolio can contain a blend of stocks and values that are ordinarily more unstable contrasted with bonds.Regardless of how long you're financial planning for, it is an outright unquestionable necessity to differentiate your portfolio. One thing is likewise without a doubt — in the event that you contribute for quite a while period you benefit from the force of compounding. This is the cycle by which the cash you make procures revenue on itself after some time. The previous you begin effective financial planning, the more you benefit from intensifying over the long haul.

Keep an eye out for high expenses

Expenses are the cash you put into somebody's pocket as opposed to your own. Despite how you contribute, you will pay expenses. What you really want to keep an eye out for is high expenses. They'll have a huge drag on your profits. You want to consider the worth you're getting in return for paying charges.

This is the way expenses influence gains on a $10,000 starting venture with a $500 month to month commitment for thirty ears (expects an arrival of 7.48%).

Investment Type	Average Mutual Fund (2.08% fee)	Automated Investing (0.5% fee)
Starting Amount	$10,000	$10,000
Year 10	$76,311	$84,508
Year 20	$140,471	$246,851
Year 30	$409,265	$486,563

Source: Wealth simple. For delineation purposes as it were. Genuine paces of return might fluctuate. Illustrative returns don't represent charges and different costs.

It's certainly worth paying an expense for an expertly planned venture portfolio that can be changed as your life altering events. It's additionally convenient to have highlights like programmed re balancing — this ensures your portfolio generally contains the right blend of resources. Some internet based speculation stages have an extraordinary mix of these administrations as well as low expenses.

The last thing you believe should do is overpay expenses. Assuming you are paying 1-2% in charges, you could lose up to 40% of your normal speculation returns after some time. Since expenses are so weighty, you ought to ensure that you're not overpaying for the help you are getting.

Consider how long you can place into investing

Dealing with your speculations(investment) can take a brief period or quite a while. Before you contribute a dollar consider how long you can place into dealing with your ventures.

A Do-It-Yourself approach will require making standard exchanges and guaranteeing sure your speculations keep focused (re-adjusting). A rob-consultant (mechanized financial planning) will cost somewhat more than doing things yourself yet it will not be as time-serious.

Make a money management arrangement/ investment plan and stick to it

Quite possibly of the main motivation numerous financial backers have low returns is on the grounds that they sell at some unacceptable time. They frequently base choices on late execution. They see what has been getting along admirably or not so well as of late. Numerous financial backers will generally purchase things that have valued in worth and sell things that have declined in esteem.

Instead of do this, you ought to make an arrangement you will assume will assist you with arriving at your objectives throughout the time span you need to contribute. Try not to quit financial planning on account of awful execution. Adhere to your arrangement without trading in view of your assessment of what will occur soon.

Assuming you're prepared to effectively utilize this multitude of fledglings contributing tips, track down a venture stage. In the event that you're pondering which one to decide, we can assist with that.

• Where should a beginner invest

6 best investments for beginners

The idea of investing can be intimidating if you're just starting out, but it's an important part of saving for various financial goals and building wealth. You'll encounter many different market environments throughout your investing life, so don't get too caught up in whether or not now is the perfect time to get started.

But before making any investment, it's important for new investors to know what their tolerance is for risk. Certain investments carry more risk than others and you don't want to be surprised after you've made the investment. Think about how long you can do without the money you'll be investing and whether you're comfortable not accessing it for a few years or longer.

Here are some top investment ideas for those just starting out.

Best investments for beginners

1. High-yield savings accounts

This can be one of the simplest ways to boost the return on your money above what you're earning in a typical checking account. High-yield savings accounts, which are often opened through an online bank, tend to pay higher interest on average than standard savings accounts while still giving customers regular access to their money.

This can be a great place to park money you're saving for a purchase in the next couple years or just holding in case of an emergency.

2. Certificates of deposit (CDs)

CDs are another way to earn additional interest on your savings, but they will tie up your money for longer than a high-yield savings account. You can purchase a CD for different time periods such as six months, one year or even five years, but you typically can't access the money before the CD matures without paying a penalty.

These are considered extremely safe and if you purchase one through a federally insured bank, you're covered up to $250,000 per depositor, per ownership category.

3. 401(k) or another workplace retirement plan

This can be one of the simplest ways to get started in investing and comes with some major incentives that could benefit you now and in the future. Most employers offer to match a portion of what you agree to save for retirement out of your regular paycheck. If your employer offers a match and you don't participate in the plan, you are turning down free money.

In a traditional 401(k), the contributions are made prior to being taxed and grow tax-free until retirement age. Some employers offer Roth 401(k)s, which allow contributions to be made after taxes. If you select this option, you won't pay taxes on withdrawals during retirement.

These workplace retirement plans are great savings tools because they're automatic once you've made your initial selections, and allow you to consistently invest over time. Often, you can even choose to invest in target-date mutual funds, which manage their portfolios based on a specific retirement date. As you get closer to the target date, the fund's allocation will shift away from riskier assets to account for a shorter investment horizon.

4. Mutual funds

Mutual funds give investors the opportunity to invest in a basket of stocks or bonds (or other assets) that they might not be able to easily build on their own.

The most popular mutual funds track indexes such as the S&P 500, which is comprised of around 500 of the largest companies in the U.S. Index funds usually come with very low fees for the funds' investors, and occasionally no fee at all. These low costs help investors keep more of the funds' returns for themselves and can be a great way to build wealth over time.

5. ETFs

Exchange-traded funds, or ETFs, are similar to mutual funds in that they hold a basket of securities, but they trade throughout the day in the same way a stock would. ETFs do not come with the same minimum investment requirements as mutual funds, which typically come in at a few thousand dollars. ETFs can be purchased for the cost of one share plus any fees or commissions associated with the purchase, though you can get started with even less if your broker allows fractional share investing.

Both ETFs and mutual funds are ideal assets to hold in tax-advantaged accounts like 401(k)s and IRAs.

6. Individual stocks

Buying stocks in individual companies is the riskiest investment option discussed here, but it can also be one of the most rewarding. But before you start making trades, you should consider whether buying a stock makes sense for you. Ask yourself if you are investing for the long-term, which generally means at least five years, and whether you understand the business you are investing in. Stocks are priced every second of the trading day and because of that, people often get drawn into the short-term trading mentality when they own individual stocks.

But a stock is a partial ownership stake in a real business and over time your fortune will rise with that of the underlying company you invested in. If you don't feel you have the expertise or stomach to ride it out with individual stocks, consider taking the more diversified approach offered by mutual funds or ETFs instead.

•How can I start investing with little as $1(for beginners)?

Investing can seem intimidating when you see experts advising workers to put away $100,000 by 35 or aim for over $1 million by retirement. But you don't need a ton of money to buy into the stock market. In some cases, you can get started with as little as $1.

Stocks and exchange-traded funds can only be bought in whole units at many brokers. Depending on the company or fund, that could mean thousands of dollars for a single share. But some financial companies are changing those requirements. Now, firms including Charles Schwab, Robinhood, Square, SoFi and Stash all allow investors to buy fractional shares of individual stocks and, in some cases, ETFs, for $1 or more.

"This is a start in the right direction," Ryan J. Marshall, a New Jersey-based certified financial planner, tells CNBC Make It. "Allowing for fractional shares of ETFs will open up the market for more investors."

If that sounds enticing, here's what to keep in mind.

Invest in mutual funds first

It's certainly positive that investing is getting cheaper on the whole for the average investor. But if you're a novice, you're going to want to stick to buying low-cost funds that track an index like the S&P 500, rather than picking and choosing individual companies to invest in.

"If you can only afford fractional shares of a stock, then you probably shouldn't purchase the stock in the first place," says Marshall.

These funds have relatively cheap fees and give you exposure to broad swaths of the stock market, which are key factors in building wealth. Stock picking by itself is a losing game — no matter how much research you put in, you're probably not going to beat the market, and studies indicates time and again that passively managed funds perform better than actively managed funds.

In today's environment, most people are running around worried about their careers, their family, what time soccer practice is on Tuesday and simply don't have the time to monitor and research individual stocks," says Marshall. "Either leave it up to mutual funds managers to make those calls or own the market in an index fund. Both provide great diversification and lower entries costs."

Buying fractional shares has always been possible when buying mutual funds, according to a spokesperson from Fidelity; it's essentially what investors do when buying into funds through a 401(k). Now, the ability to buy fractional shares is expanding to ETFs and stocks too, which you'd typically buy through a taxable brokerage account.

"The individual investor is better suited by investing in mutual funds and exchange-traded funds," Greg McBride, chief financial analyst at Bankrate, told CNBC Make It. "But the lure of individual stocks is always there. On some level, so is the belief that doing so enables the investor to beat the market, which has proven not to be true."

Then buy individual stocks

That said, if you're already contributing a healthy amount to a retirement investment account like a 401(k) or IRA but want to dip your toe into individual stock trading, buying fractional shares can be a good starting point.

This way, you can invest in expensive companies like Amazon or Alphabet without the near-$2,000 necessary to buy a single share (Amazon was trading for close to $1,900 on Friday; Alphabet was at just over $1,400). It's also an effective way for to test out a company before committing a large amount of money.

Again, it shouldn't be your sole investing strategy, but if you want to build on your retirement accounts, it's a good entry point. CNBC's Jim Cramer says the first $10,000 you invest should go to a low-cost index fund or exchange-traded fund that mirrors the S&P 500.

After that, you can start researching individual companies to invest in if that's part of your overall financial plan and you have the time and   resources   to   do   so.

3

STOCK AND SHARE

•WHAT ARE STOCK AND SHARE(OFFER)

A large number of us accept that money is a protected approach to saving. It is to be sure vital to have an effectively available 'stormy day' reserve - yet with expansion rates increasing, your money investment funds could before long beginning losing esteem. On the off chance that you're stressed over that, putting resources into a stocks and offers ISA can offer the potential for better returns, assisting you with beating expansion.

Yet, large numbers of us likewise stress over the difficulties of money management. It can appear to be extremely complicated and confounding. The worth of any venture can go down as well as up, so you could wind up losing cash as opposed to saving it. As a matter of fact our new exploration shows that 18% of us are terrified of making some unacceptable venture decisions 1.

As Emma Byron, Overseeing Head of Legitimate and General Retirement Arrangements, says:

"Knowing where to begin is hard - particularly in violent times. Individuals will justifiably be having an uncertain outlook on the future right now." However she proceeds to make a consoling point: "The vital thing to recall is that contributing is as long as possible. With time on your side, you might possibly adjust the highs and lows of the market."

We will expand on her recommendation in this article. We'll make sense of some fundamental venture ideas and present a decent starter speculation item: the Stocks and Offers ISA. That will assist you with choosing if you have any desire to contribute your reserve funds and ideally set you headed for progress assuming you do.

What are stocks and shares(offers)?

Stocks and offers are units of possession in an organization. Organizations offer them to investors to give financing to develop their business. A few organizations have a great many investors, who all own a little piece of the organization; others have quite recently a small bunch. Individuals trade shares on securities exchanges like the London Stock Trade (LSE).

How stocks and shares can beat inflation

There are two different ways for investors to "acquire" cash:

Selling their portions at a greater expense than they paid for them

Clutching their portions as a trade-off for a payout from the organization, known as a profit.

That can make a return that is higher than the pace of inflation, which is the way the right speculation can assist you with beating inflation .

Obviously assuming there are worries about the organization's development or execution and interest for shares is low, the worth of your portions will go down and you might get back short of what you contributed. There's no assurance on profits by the same token. In an unfortunate year, the chiefs might conclude there isn't sufficient cash for a payout. As Emma says, consistently worth recalling effective financial planning is as long as possible.

The most effective method to put resources into the securities exchange

There are three methods for putting resources into the securities exchange. You can:

Pick the singular offers yourself

Utilize a specialist to pick the offers for you

Contribute through a speculation store, where an asset chief picks the offers for every one of the financial backers in the asset.

Wise speculations for amateurs

There's a lot to consider in the event that you're new to money management, as:

How high to set your spending plan

How long you're probably going to contribute

Your mentality to risk

The amount you're willing to lose in the event that circumstances don't pan out.

A stocks and offers ISA could be an extraordinary spot to begin. It's a straightforward, simple to-utilize speculation item that can assist you with seeing more about the financial exchange and how ventures work after some time.

"The ideal choice will rely upon individual situation, yet we see a genuine requirement for a straightforward venture item. That is the reason we're sending off a minimal expense and basic Stocks and Offers ISA to carry more decision to savers who know that their reserve funds are being influenced by expansion and low financing costs, however they don't have the foggiest idea what to do about it," says Emma.

Like any venture, your ISA's worth could fall as well as rise and isn't ensured. You might get back short of what you contribute, particularly over a more limited timeframe.

The most effective method to put resources into stocks for amateurs with minimal expenditure

In the event that you don't have a major singular amount, you can in any case contribute. Our Stocks and Offers ISA can be opened with a £100 singular amount or just £20 each month, making it a truly available method for beginning money management.

The more you contribute, the more you could find consequently. However, recall, with higher potential returns comes more vulnerability, so you ought to ensure you select the gamble level that turns out best for you.

How much are stocks and shares(offers)ISA charges?

Each supplier sets their own expenses. These will frequently cover dealing with your assets and will likewise rely upon whether you have decided to utilize a monetary counselor. For the most part, the charges will be founded on:

The amount you have contributed

Administration and asset charge

It might likewise bring about exchange costs.

Our yearly charge will be deducted directly from your venture, so you won't have to stress over paying for it through direct charges or yearly exchanges. Our ISA expenses number cruncher will show you how much our yearly Stocks and Offers ISA charges will be.

What other ISA choices are accessible?

You can likewise place your cash into other ISA choices, including:

Cash ISA

Advancement ISA

Lifetime ISA (assuming you're matured 18-39)

You can place your cash into a mix of every one of the four ISAs, as long as you don't contribute more than the ISA yearly remittance or open more than one of each fiscal year. We at present just proposition a stocks and share(offers)ISA.

•Where to Purchase Stocks

More often than not, stocks are recorded and exchanged on trades, authorized scenes where purchasers and dealers meet, frequently with the help of a specialist or other go-between. These mediators will be individuals from the trade and utilize their admittance to trade shares for your sake. Significant trades in the US incorporate the New York Stock Trade (NYSE) and the Nasdaq market.

More modest organizations with less fluid offers and negligible market covers (at times called penny stocks) may on the other hand exchange over-the-counter (OTC) on additional inexactly managed stages like the OTC Pink Sheets. Portions of these organizations are much of the time more unstable and dangerous, so financial backers deciding to exchange on the OTC market ought to participate in extra reasonable level of effort and comprehend the dangers implied.

KEY Focal points

To exchange stocks, you'll frequently have to utilize a representative to put in your requests on a trade.

A full-administration merchant, while more costly, gives master speculation examination, exhortation, and editorial notwithstanding thorough monetary preparation.

A markdown representative is a less expensive choice that gives essential execution administrations to financial backers who do their own examination and investigation.

Today, numerous internet based agents offer sans commission exchanging alongside free instruments and screeners, making it simpler than any time in recent memory to exchange stocks on

Purchasing Stocks With a Full-Administration Representative

Full-administration representatives certain individuals imagine when they ponder putting — fashionable money managers sitting in an office and visiting with clients. These are the customary stockbrokers who will carve out opportunity to get to know you actually and monetarily.

They will take a gander at variables like conjugal status, way of life, character, risk resilience, age (time skyline), pay, resources, obligations, and that's just the beginning.

1

By getting to be aware as much about you as possible, these full-administration intermediaries or brokers can then assist you with fostering a drawn out monetary arrangement.

These merchants or brokers can assist you with your venture needs as well as furnish help with domain arranging, charge exhortation, retirement arranging, planning, and some other kind of monetary counsel — thus the expression "full assistance." They can assist you with dealing with each of your monetary necessities now and long into the future and are for financial backers who need everything in one bundle.

As far as charges, full-administration intermediaries or brokers are more costly than markdown representatives, yet the benefit of having an expert human venture consultant close by can be certainly worth the extra expenses. Accounts today can be set up with just $1,000. A great many people, particularly novices, would fall into this class regarding the sort of brokers whom they require.

The people who need a set-it-and-forget-it way to deal with financial planning yet don't have the cash or time to recruit a full-administration specialist can pick a roboadvisor. These are algorithmic speculation stages that you can oversee through an application or site for a small part of the expense of a customary monetary guide.

Purchasing Stocks On the web

On the web/rebate merchants, then again, give no speculation guidance and are essentially request takers. They are significantly less costly than full-administration representatives, since there is regularly no office to visit and no ensured venture consultants to help you. Cost is generally founded on a for every exchange premise, and you can commonly open a record over the Web with practically zero cash. When you have a record with an internet based merchant, you can generally sign on to its site and into your record and have the option to immediately trade stocks.

Recollect that since these sorts of agents give definitely no venture exhortation, stock tips, or speculation help of any sort, you're all alone to deal with your speculations. The main help that you will as a rule get is specialized help. On the web (markdown) specialists truly do offer venture related connections, exploration, and assets that can be valuable. Assuming you feel that you are sufficiently educated to assume the obligations of dealing with your own speculations, or on the other hand if you realize nothing about money management except for need to show yourself, then this is the best approach.

Basically your decision of dealer ought to be founded on your singular necessities. Full-administration representatives are perfect for the people who will pay a premium for another person to take care of their funds. On the web/rebate agents, then again, are perfect for individuals with little beginning up cash and who might want to face the dangers challenges prizes of money management upon themselves, with no expert help.

Purchasing Stocks By means of an Immediate Stock Buy Plan

Once in a while, organizations (frequently blue-chip firms) will support an exceptional sort of program called an immediate stock buy plan (DSPP).

2

DSPPs were initially considered ages prior as a way for organizations to allow more modest financial backers to purchase possession straightforwardly from the organization. Taking part in a DSPP requires a financial backer to draw in with an organization straightforwardly rather than with a merchant, however every organization's framework for overseeing a DSPP is novel.

Taking an interest organizations will offer their DSPP through move specialists or another outsider manager. To get familiar with how to take part in an organization's DSPP, a financial backer ought to contact the organization's financial backer relations office.

How to Trade Once You Have a Broker

Once you've chosen your brokerage platform, you will need to establish and fund an account before you can begin trading. Today, it's easier than ever to link a bank account online and transfer funds, or to electronically roll over an existing brokerage account to another firm. You can also choose to make recurring deposits into your brokerage account to increase your portfolio on a regular basis.

Once funded, you simply need to go online or call your broker to place a trade. Stocks are designated by a unique ticker symbol, a one- to four-letter mnemonic assigned to a particular company. MSFT, for instance, is the ticker for Microsoft Inc., and AAPL is the ticker for Apple Inc. If you don't know the ticker of your stock, it is easy to look it up online or via your broker.

When you select the stock ticker that you would like to trade, you'll be met with a price quote, a set of information about the stock's price and activity. This will show you the last price at which the shares traded, as well as a bid and an offer. The bid is the highest price at which somebody in the market will buy a share (and thus is the best price at which you can sell to them). The offer, or ask, is the lowest price at which somebody in the market is willing to sell (and thus, it's the best price at which you can buy from them). The difference between the bid and offer prices is known as the spread. A narrower spread typically indicates that the market for the stock is quite active and liquid. A wider spread indicates the opposite. After considering the price quote, you may place your order.

Market orders are the most basic type of order and will give you immediate execution at the prevailing market price. A limit order, on the other hand, allows you to set a specific price at which to buy or sell. If the price never reaches that limit level, then the trade will remain active until it is canceled. Many such trades are day orders that will remain good until the end of the trading day. If you want the order to be active only briefly, you can instead specify with your broker that it is immediate or cancel (IOC). Alternatively, if you want the order to remain in force for longer than a day, then you can designate it good 'til canceled (GTC). Other conditions can also be placed on an order, such as a stop-loss.

Once your trade is executed (in whole or in part), you will receive a fill—a summary of your order's details.

How Old Do You Have to be to Trade Stocks?

You must be at least 18 years old in the United States to open a brokerage account and trade stocks.

3

For somebody younger than 18, a parent can set up a custodial account on their behalf.

Is It Possible to Buy and Sell Stocks for Free?

Yes. Several online brokerage platforms (such as Robinhood) offer commission-free trading in most stocks and exchange-traded funds (ETFs). Note that these brokers still earn money from your trades, but by selling order flow to financial firms and loaning your stock to short-sellers.

What Is the Easiest Way to Buy Stock?

The easiest way, in terms of getting a trade done, is to open and fund an online account and place a market order. While this is the quickest way to buy stocks, it might not always be the wisest. Do your own research before deciding what type of order to place and with whom.

Do You Need a Broker to Buy Stocks?

Some publicly traded companies offer a direct stock purchase plan (DSPP), where you can buy shares directly. Instead of using a broker, the company's transfer agent manages the transaction.

The Bottom Line

You can buy or sell stock on your own by opening a brokerage account with one of the many brokerage firms. After opening your account, connect it with your bank checking account to make deposits, which are then available for you to invest in.

However, do not equate the ease of opening an account with the ease of making good investment decisions. It is generally recommended that beginners speak to a qualified financial advisor. New investors might benefit from reading the key book The Intelligent Investor, by Benjamin Graham. Smart investing can be highly satisfying, so take it slow, do your research, and seek out a broker that suits your interests and goals.

- **stock exchange's**

Stock exchange definition

What is a stock exchange?

A stock exchange is a centralised location where the shares of publicly traded companies are bought and sold. Stock exchanges differ from other exchanges because the tradable assets are limited to stocks, bonds and exchange traded products (ETPs).

The main difference between using a stock exchange and over-the-counter (OTC) methods of trading stocks is that, on an exchange, transactions are mediated rather than taking place directly between two parties. This means that there are stricter regulations on investors and speculators, as well as on the companies listed.

Companies often need to meet specific standards before they can be listed on a stock exchange – these standards can vary depending on the stock exchange. For example, the NASDAQ requires companies to have a market value of $70 million before they can be listed, whereas the New York Stock Exchange requires a company's value to be $100 million.

•Examples of stock exchanges or stock trades

There are various stock trades all over the planet. Probably the biggest trades are the New York Stock Trade (NYSE), the NASDAQ, and the Tokyo Stock Trade (JPX). Other notable stock trades incorporate the London Stock Trade (LSE), the Shanghai Stock Trade (SSE) and the Bombay Stock Trade (BSE).

Advantages and disadvantages of stock trades

Stock trades have a scope of upsides and downsides for both the organizations that are recorded on them, and for the people trying to exchange on them.

Stars of stock trades

For an organization, being recorded on a stock trade accompanies a specific degree of glory. This is especially valid for more seasoned trades, like Amsterdam, London and New York. Being recorded on a trade likewise implies financial backers can purchase partakes in the organization, which assists the organization with growing by raising assets.

By exchanging on a stock trade, it is reasonable merchants will be at less gamble of counterparty default. This is because of the great degrees of guideline on stock trades, which is something that OTC strategies for exchanging need.

Moreover, online business firms have made it significantly simpler for brokers to get to stock trades and gain the chance to benefit from any momentary market developments.

Cons of stock trades

For an organization, posting on a stock trade can be tedious and costly. What's more, when the organization has recorded, it should consider its liability to investors, who currently have a stake in the organization.

Exchanging on a stock trade doesn't ensure strength. Securities exchanges are defenseless to showcase unpredictability, and that intends that there can be sensational swings in the cost of stock, generally in light of political and monetary occasions all over the planet.

Stock trades can likewise encounter crashes. Despite the fact that they are intriguing, financial exchange accidents can fundamentally decrease the worth of stocks and lead to financial downturns that keep going for quite a long time.

Brokers and financial backers can deal with their openness to securities exchange instability by carrying out a gamble the board technique

4

STOCK DIVIDEND

•What is a Stock Dividend or Stock Profit?

A stock profit which is also know as stock dividend,a technique utilized by organizations to convey abundance to investors, is a profit installment made as offers instead of money. Stock profits are essentially given in lieu of money profits when the organization is coming up short on fluid money available. The governing body settles on when to proclaim a (stock) profit and in what structure the profit will be paid.

Effect of a Stock Profit/ Stock Dividend on Market Capitalization

Like a money profit, a stock profit doesn't increment investor riches or market capitalization. Despite the fact that it builds the quantity of offers remarkable for an organization, the cost per share should diminish likewise. A comprehension that the market capitalization of an organization continues as before makes sense of why offer cost should diminish in the event that more offers are given. The accompanying outline delineates the idea:

	No Dividend	10% Stock Dividend
Shares Owned	1,000	1,100
Price Per Share	$ 10.00	$ 9.09
Total Value	$ 10,000	$ 10,000

Example of a Stock Dividend

Colin is a shareholder of ABC Company and owns 1,000 shares. The board of directors of ABC Company recently announced a 10% stock dividend. Assuming that the current stock price is $10 and there are 100,000 total shares outstanding, what is the effect of a 10% stock dividend on Colin's 1,000 shares?

1. Determine the market capitalization of ABC Company:

$10 x 100,000 shares = $1,000,000 (market capitalization)

2. Determine the increase in shares outstanding due to a 10% stock dividend:

100,000 shares x 10% = 10,000 increase in shares outstanding

3. Determine the new total shares outstanding:

10,000 + 100,000 = 110,000 shares

4. Determine the number of shares Colin now owns:

Before the stock dividend, Colin owned 1% (1,000 / 100,000) of the total outstanding shares. Since a stock dividend is given to all shareholders, Colin's ownership percentage in ABC Company remains the same.

Therefore, Colin would own 1% of the new total shares outstanding or 1% x 110,000 = 1,100. The number is identical to increasing Colin's 1,000 shares by the 10% stock dividend.

5. Determine the price per share of ABC Company:

A stock dividend does not increase the market capitalization of a company. The market capitalization of ABC Company remains $1,000,000. With 110,000 total shares outstanding, the stock price of ABC Company would be $1,000,000 / 110,000 = $9.09.

The following diagram illustrates the impact of a stock dividend on Colin:

	No Dividend	10% Stock Dividend
Shares Outstanding	100,000	110,000
Price Per Share	$ 10.00	$ 9.09
Market Capitalization	$ 1,000,000	$ 1,000,000

The following diagram illustrates the impact of a stock dividend on ABC Company:

Example: Consider a company with a market capitalization of $1,000,000 and 100,000 shares outstanding

Stock Dividend of ...	Shares Outstanding	Share Price	Market Capitalization
N/A	100,000	$ 10.00	$ 1,000,000
5%	105,000	$ 9.52	$ 1,000,000
10%	110,000	$ 9.09	$ 1,000,000
15%	115,000	$ 8.70	$ 1,000,000
20%	120,000	$ 8.33	$ 1,000,000
25%	125,000	$ 8.00	$ 1,000,000
50%	150,000	$ 6.67	$ 1,000,000
100%	200,000	$ 5.00	$ 1,000,000

The key takeaway from our example is that a stock dividend does not affect the total value of the shares that each shareholder holds in the company. As the number of shares increases, the price per share decreases accordingly because the market capitalization must remain the same.

•Advantages of a Stock Dividend

1. Keeping up with cash position

An organization that needs more money might decide to deliver a stock profit in lieu of a money profit. As such, a money profit permits an organization to keep up with its ongoing money position.

2. Charge contemplation for a stock profit

No duty contemplation exist for giving a stock profit. Thus, investors commonly accept that a stock profit is better than a money profit - a money profit is treated as pay in the year got and is, hence, burdened.

3. Keeping an "invest able" cost range

As indicated over, a stock profit builds the quantity of offers while likewise diminishing the offer cost. By bringing down the offer cost through a stock profit, an organization's stock might be more "reasonable" to the general population.

For instance, consider a financial backer with $1,000 hoping to put resources into Stock An or Stock B. Stock An is estimated at $2,000 while Stock B is evaluated at $500. Stock A would be considered "excessively expensive" for the financial backer since he just has $1,000 to contribute.

Weaknesses of a Stock Profit

1. Market flagging and deviated data

The market might see a stock profit as a lack of money, flagging monetary issues. Market members might accept the organization is monetarily upset, as they don't have the foggiest idea about the genuine justification behind administration giving a stock profit. This can come down on the stock and push down its cost.

2. Hazardous activities

Giving a stock profit rather than a money profit might flag that the organization is utilizing its money to put resources into dangerous ventures. The training can raise questions about the organization's administration and in this manner push down its stock cost.

Diary Sections for a Stock Profit

The diary passages for a stock profit relies upon whether the organization is engaged with a little stock profit or a huge stock profit. The diary passages for the two sizes are represented underneath:

1. Little profit/dividend

A stock profit or dividend is viewed as a little stock profit on the off chance that the quantity of offers being given is under 25%. For instance, expect an organization holds 5,000 normal offers extraordinary and proclaims a 5% normal stock profit. Also, the standard worth per stock is $1, and the market esteem is $10 on the announcement date. In this situation, 5,000 x 5% = 250 new normal offers will be given. The accompanying passages are made:

On Declaration Date		
Dr. Retained Earnings (250 shares x $10 market value)	$2,500	
Cr. Common Stock Dividend Distributable (250 shares x $1 par value)		$250
Cr. Additional Paid-in Capital - Common Stock		$2,250
On Distribution of Stock Dividend		
Dr. Common Stock Dividend Distributable	$250	
Cr. Common Stock		$250

2. Large dividend

A stock dividend is considered a large stock dividend if the number of shares being issued is greater than 25%. For example, assume a company owns 5,000 common shares outstanding and declares a 50% common stock dividend. In addition, the par value per stock is $1, and the market value is $10 on the declaration date. In such a scenario, 5,000 x 50% = 2,500 new common shares will be issued. The following entries are made:

On Declaration Date		
Dr. Retained Earnings (2,500 shares x $1 par value)	$2,500	
Cr. Common Stock Dividend Distributable		$2,500

On Distribution of Stock Dividend		
Dr. Common Stock Dividend Distributable	$2,500	
Cr. Common Stock		$2,500

Benefits Of Stick Dividend:Stock dividend give you more than you think.

When talking about the stock market Most investors often think of it as a lucrative business in order to get the fastest profit. That may not be the right strategy for long-term investment. If you want to create sustainable wealth. You have to let money works for you. And one of the strategies to invest money to work for us is to invest in stock dividend

Why invest with stock dividend?

The principle of investing in a stock that investors often forget is investing in stocks is an investment in a business. No matter what business it is. It is a business that operates with managers, employees, customers, products and services. The only hope is that the profits from the business. (It's not just the 3-4 characters you will print in Set trade, just to check stock prices.) What we will get as a return on equity is dividends, if we choose to invest in good business. Highly competitive business will be profitable and continue to grow. That will be able to increase the wealth to the shareholders quite well.

In addition, investment in stock dividend can beat inflation. The basic inflation in Thailand's economy is about 3% per year. If we consider that investment in stocks is an investment in the business. When we invest in good business. The business expects growth. On average, the growth rate of a good company is often more than inflation. Investing in stocks gives you an average return of 5-10% per year, which can be easily beaten by inflation.

How do we invest in stock dividend?

Stock dividend selection Three major factors are considered to select stock dividend

1. Should have a strong financial position. Be a leader in the business. Have a brand or brand that is remembered by customers. We need to know and understand the business we are investing in. Regularity in dividends This reflects the Company's policy and rigor in paying dividends. It may be based on past dividend payout data. Dividend stocks are good but dividend should pay more each year. For example, from the first year's first dividend of 1 baht, second year should be dividend of 1.10 baht, and third year should be dividend of 1.20 baht. If the company can pay more dividends that means the financial health and operations of the company are likely to continue to grow. It will give the capitalist a degree of peace of mind.

2. Do not forget that investment in dividends is a long-term investment to make money work for us. In addition, we often find that after the company pays dividends. The stock price is equal to or greater than the dividend we have. (Dividend payment to shareholders is payout comes from net profit or retained earnings, resulting in a decrease in cash flow.) As a result, if we expect only short-term dividends then just want to buy shares to receive dividends and then sell it. This may cause us losses at stock prices instead.

3. Investing in dividend stocks also risk that must be aware of. The dividends that are now seen are based on past performance and the past did not indicate the future. If investors use only statistical numbers such as dividends in the past then come to invest for the return of dividends. It is unlikely that they will get the expected return. Sometimes

when the company wants to use capital to expand business, the company may not be able to pay dividends as much as it already has.

So what investors should do is study the business (stock) we want to invest. Assess future profitability trends which is the best signal to say that the company has a chance to pay dividends continuously? And keep track and investigate our investments consistently. If this is done. Your next stock dividend will have a higher chance of success.

5

SHARES, AN INVESTMENT FOR LIFE

•THE SHARES, AN INVESTMENT FOR LIFE

Your best option to a convenient and stable financial life in future is to embrace equity/share investment. Who should invest? The answer is everyone. But you cannot invest unless you save and saving is a function of income.Income: In economics income is defined as a function of consumption and saving (i.e. income = consumption + saving), and equate saving to investment (i.e. saving = investment). Now the questions are?Do you have income?Is your income enough to meet critical needs i.e. basic needs of life?What do you do with the excess of your income?Consumption: Questions of people today is "where is the excess?" The truth is that in every income, there is always an excess provided the earner wants to live within his means. In a situation where income is equal to consumption, the earner has no plan for tomorrow. Someone once said that there is always that small reckless spending in every income no matter how little the income is. You can prove this by writing down your expenses and income for the month. You will be surprised to see how much you consume and how less you save. You cannot save unless you discipline yourself. Thus to save for investment, you must check your consumption.Saving: This is the excess of income over consumption. The beginning of personal wealth is the capital that you can use for investing. This capital often begins with saving and expands into other types of more profitable investment. Saving is the beginning of your capital accumulation. Families need a regular saving program that's between 5 and 10 percent of take home pay per month. Some people manage to put away 15 percent. Getting into a regular rhythm with saving is important. Remember we cannot have all our wants (not needs); hence there is need for sacrifice. When we curtail our consumption, we would be able to save and then invest. Additionally, individuals and families need emergency funds . This is money for any unexpected expenses that may arise. Investment: The use of money through various vehicles, to make more income or increase capital (capital gain). It is also buying or sacrificing something today, with the intent of creating a stream of wealth in the future Types of investment: There are various means of investment. Individuals can have one, all or mix of these investments. The issue will therefore be what is the investment motive? Your small or large savings can be invested in any of the following:

1. Money Market instruments like:Fixed deposit Treasury bills Treasury Certificate Negotiable Certificate of Deposits Commercial papers

2. Capital Market instruments like:Ordinary shares Preference stocks

Long Term Loan Federal/State/Local Government Bonds Industrial Loans

3. Life assurance policies

4. Real Estate or assets

5. Commodities (agriculture or Minerals)The type of investment depends on your financial capabilities, expert advice and your attitude towards risk- risk lover, risk averted or risk neutral.

All investments have their advantages and disadvantages while the returns and the risks vary from one to another.Investing in shares A share is just what it says it is – a share of a company. When you buy a share you become a part-owner (a shareholder) of a company. Being part-owner or a shareholder means that you share in the profits of the company. Other names for shares are equities and stocks.Companies issue shares. These shares represent the money which shareholders (as part-owners of the company) put down when they first invest in the company.Owners of shares (shareholders) own the company. If the company makes a profit, the shareholders have a right to a share of the profit. We call such a slice of the profit a dividend. A dividend is not a fixed amount. Each year the directors of the company make two important recommendations about profits made by the company.

1. Firstly, they recommend what slice of the profit the company should keep in reserve for future expansion.

2. Secondly, they recommend what slice of the profit the company should pay out to its shareholders.The profit the company makes for the year determines how big each slice will be.

Shares are traded on the US Stock Exchange during every working day of the year.

How do I buy shares?

1. Buying New Shares (Primary market): As an investor you can buy shares from a company during its initial public offer (to be traded on the stock exchange for the first time) or an existing company issuing new shares to increase its paid up capital (Rights and Public Offer). To buy shares in a new issue, you simply fill in the application form in the prospectus, and send it with a cheque to the address given. Issues in primary market are always cheaper since charges in the secondary market are absent and the offer price is always lower than the market price. Share Certificates will be issued to the successful investors. Your share certificate or certificate of holding shows how many shares you own. It is an important document and will be needed when you want to sell the shares. You can also use itas collateral for loans in a bank or any financial institution.

2. Buying existing shares (secondary market): Shares can also be bought on the floor of the stock exchange from existing shareholders. To buy shares in the secondary market, you have to appoint a stock broker, who is a licensed dealer of the exchange. A stock broker provides a personal service to meet an individual's specific need. You can buy any quantity of shares but at the prevailing market price. A contract note showing the details of the transaction carried out is given to the investor by the stockbroker. A CSCS (Central Securities Clearing system) statement showing the stock position is also given to the investor through the stockbroker on a monthly basis. Motives for buying shares: Every investor has a personal reason for investing in shares . For example In order to have a regular income for sustenance during retirement period For capital appreciation or growth In order to have ownership stake in a company or to gain control of the company by being elected to the Board of Directors The motives for buying shares can be long term or short term Long Term – Shares can be bought in large or small quantities at regular intervals over a period of time in order to meet a particular need in future. The most important thing is that the fund is expected to have grown to a target value top meet the need. The investor has no intention to sell the shares on the short run but to collect regular dividends and bonus regularly. Retirement schemes and pension funds schemes adopt this approach. "The valuation or worth of the investment of a young graduate who started working in 1995 and caught the vision of buying shares is as shown below. He invested $35,000 to purchase 9,000 units of merchant bank at the rate of $3.75 per share.

Year	Initial unit	Bonus recieved	Bonus unit	Total holdings
1995	9000	1:4	2,250	11,250
1996		1:4	2,812	14,062
1997		1:4	3,515	17,189
1998		1:4	4,394	21,225
1999		1:4	5,492	27,551
2000		1:4	6,865	30,216
2001		1:4	8,582	35,782
2002		1:4	8,582	42,572
2003		1:5	8,582	54,271
2004		1:8	6,436	58,789

At the current average price of $23.00 per share, this young graduate is worth$1,332,344.00. This scenario is excluding dividends received by the investment up to date

The truth to learn are

1. Some of us had more money than the graduate had at that period.

2. The sum of $35,000.00 looked small that it could have been spent on clothes, jewelries, entertainment etc

3.If he loses his job today, he can still survive the next six months without hassle pending the time he sorts himself out. Of course he can start a business of his own with this sum and become great in the process". (Figure extracts from Winning Battle Against Poverty via Investment in US Capital Market by Carlos fray) Short term - Shares can also be bought for short term capital gain. It is speculative in nature and sometimes called trading. Here your money is working for you. This involves buying when the price of a share is low and selling when the price is high. It is a function of timing. It entails the analysis and forecast of the market by an analyst/expert. Here the higher the risk the higher the return.

•Risks and how to manage it

you can't eliminate risk when you invest, but you can understand it and take steps to keep it at acceptable levels. Risk is an inevitable component of investing. It is necessary to accept a certain amount of risk in order to generate a reasonable return on your investment. The more risk you're willing to take, the greater the potential return your investment can provide.

The amount of risk you should take is dependent on the two primary factors: your personal tolerance and your time frame. It is important to understand how much risk you can accept in your own investing. It is not a good sign if you are constantly worried about your investment portfolio and fearful of what will happen if share prices fall. You should be comfortable with the risk level of assets you own, whether you are investing on your own or following the advice of a financial planner. A good rule of thumb is if you can pass the sleep test. If you stare at the ceiling from your bed each night, thinking of how you will cope if the market crashes, taking your portfolio along with it, then you have probably invested in assets that are too risky for your personal comfort. You should reduce your risk exposure until you own a portfolio that allows you to sleep at night.

•Risk reduction strategies

1. Diversify.

Financial advisors generally agree that most types of risk can be managed by diversification i.e. dividing your investments among different industries and asset classes (stocks, bonds, real estate, etc.). "Spreading the risk" through diversification helps cushion the impact that problems in one investment might have on a portfolio (a portfolio is a collection of investments). Mutual funds have become popular investment vehicles partly because they enable individual investors, who often lack the resources and expertise to achieve adequate diversification on their own, to gain instant diversification through a professionally managed portfolio. For example, a fund like the Discovery Fund can invest at least 25% of its assets in income-producing securities to offset the higher risk of its stock-market holdings. And within its stock portfolio, the Fund diversifies among various industries to spread the market risk further.

2. Be patient.

Research has shown that very high stock-market returns occur only over short periods. On the other hand, losses disappear almost completely over ten-year holding periods, and they vanish over 20-year holding periods. The message: to reduce risk, invest for the long term.

3. Jump in gradually.

Lump-sum investing can produce spectacular returns - if your timing is right. That's a big "if." Few professional investors consistently "time" the market correctly, and individual investors are notorious for timing it incorrectly, buying at a high price and selling at a low price. For most investors, investing a fixed amount of money on, say, a monthly basis provides a disciplined approach that can reduce investment risks and improve long-term returns.One of the greatest investment risks is the risk of not investing. Yes, it is true, investing has a risk of loss, and no one person can guarantee you a return, if any at all. However, the risk of not investing has at least one guaranteed outcome, and that is NOT achieving an investment return. No capital growth. No passive income. Not achieving your financial goals. It makes more sense to invest and educate yourself on ways to mitigate the risks rather than to sit back and do nothing and therefore not to invest.

6

REAL ESTATE

What Exactly Is Real Estate

Definition: Real estate investing refers to the purchase of property as an investment to generate income rather than using it as a primary residence. In simple terms, it can be understood as any land, building, infrastructure and other tangible property which is usually immovable but transferable.

Some of the examples of real estate are a house, office building, agricultural land, commercial plot, etc. It is considered to be a secured form of investment.

Classification of Real Estate

Real estate includes various properties which can be classified by their uses. These are as follows:

Content: Real Estate Investing

- Classification

- Features

- Means

- Benefits

- Drawbacks

- Reasons for Failure

- Tips

- Classification of Real Estate

Residential Real Estate: The real estate which consists of home, i.e., single, duplex, triplex, township, bungalow etc. used for residential purpose. Whether it is a newly constructed property or a house to be resold by the owner.

Industrial Real Estate: A large scale property utilized to build factories, manufacturing units, warehouses, distribution centers, etc. are categorized under industrial real estate.

Commercial Real Estate: The properties or office buildings such as a complex, are parted into multiple small units. These are rented out or used to run various businesses. Therefore, they are known as commercial real estate.

Retail Space: These properties are used as showrooms, restaurants, shopping malls, retail stores, etc. either individual units or multiple units located in the prime location.

Land: Any vacant land where activities like ranching or farming take place is also a form of real estate.

Fix and Flip Properties: The residential properties which are in a poorly maintained state and are available at a low price are termed as the fix and flip properties. These properties, when purchased by the buyers involved in renovation and repairs of properties to modify them and sell at a high price.

Mixed-Use: A single high-end real estate project which constitutes of different types of properties mentioned above to ensure diversification and minimize the risk of project failure, is termed under mixed-use real estate.

Features of Real Estate Investing

When we talk about real estate, we can say that it requires a lot of foresightedness and capital investment to expect fruitful returns.

Let us now understand the characteristics of real estate investment one by one:

Features of Real Estate Investing

Tangible: Real estate or properties are one of those investments which have a physical existence and can be touched and seen.

Immune to Inflation: When economic inflation creates a negative impact on the value of other investments, investing in real estate is a fruitful option. It is the only investment which results in value appraisal in adverse situations.

Allows Use of Leverage: The financial institutions are attracted towards funding for real estate because of its real or physical existence.

Uncertain Maturity Period: Real estate investment does not have any fixed maturity period like in other investments such as fixed deposits and bonds. It is the owner who decides whether to hold the property or sell it.

Value Enhancement: Investing in properties can provide dual benefit to the investors. On the one hand, real estate generates rental income, and on the other hand, its value keeps on increasing in the long run.

Low Liquidity: One of the essential features of real estate is that it is a capital asset. Therefore, it cannot be frequently bought or sold like stocks or equity.

Needs Management: Real estate investment is buying a physical asset which involves the expenditure on its maintenance. The investor also needs to manage the source of income so generated.

Universally Acceptable as Collateral: Financing the properties by taking them as collateral is very common among the banks and other financial institutions.

Profitable Even During Recession: Real estate investments have been considered as one of the safest investments. If done wisely, they yield profit or generate income even at the time of recession.

Means of Earning Through Real Estate

To make money from real estate, one has various options. The significant ways of investing in real estate are mentioned below:

Means of Earning Through Real Estate

Appreciation of Property Value: Usually, the value of property keeps on increasing even in the situation of inflation in the economy, therefore investing in real estate is a wise decision.

Rental Income: Renting out premises, whether residential or commercial, is always a good idea for generating a progressive passive income in the long run.

Related Commission: The real estate management companies, agents or brokers can make money in the form of commission by facilitating the exchange of property among the buyer and the seller.

Income from Ancillary Real Estate Investment: Other than regular income from business or salary, one can develop a source of additional revenue by various means. One of these is installing a vending machine in the running business premises.

Real Estate Investment Trusts (REIT): In India, the investors who are willing to invest in the real estate but lack sufficient capital can buy units of real estate investment trusts, listed with the stock exchange and approved by SEBI. The fund so collected are invested in different types of real estate projects.

Benefits of Investing in Real Estate

Investment in real estate can prove to be beneficial in the long run. If done wisely, it may generate lucrative returns.

The advantages of pooling money in real estate are as follows:

Benefits of Investing in Real Estate

Hedge Against Inflation: Unlike other assets, real estate is not adversely affected by inflation. Instead, its value and income increase with the rising economy.

Rent Pays Off for Mortgage: Residential and commercial properties are the only assets which have the capability of generating income through rentals to pay off the interest on their mortgage.

Stable Income: It can be seen as the most significant source of generating passive income. The investors can rent out their property to ensure regular and steady cash inflow.

Tax Benefits: Real estate investors relish tax exemptions on the rental income up to a specific limit. Even the tax rates for such investments when made for the long term, are quite low.

Self Decision Making: A real estate investor is free to make his or her own decision, similar to running any other business entity. In short, the investor is his or her boss.

Financial Security: As we know that putting money in real estate is a long term investment. The investor has the possession of a physical asset, hence providing financial security to the person.

Value Appreciation: Real estate investment is the purchase of property which encounters capital appreciation in the long run.

Drawbacks of Investing in Real Estate

When real estate is a profitable investment, it has some limitations which are discussed below:

Drawbacks of Investing in Real Estate

High Maintenance and Management: Real estate investment is buying a physical asset which involves the expenditure on its maintenance. The investor also needs to manage the source of income so generated.

Huge Transaction Cost: Buying and selling of properties is a costly affair. The transaction cost, including registry charges, legal expenses, diversion, etc. are so high that the cost of investment increases for the buyer.

Creates Financial and Legal Liability: The investor may become overburdened by the financial liability if he or she buys a property on loan. Even the transfer of ownership at the time of property purchase creates a legal obligation on the investor.

Less Liquid in Nature: Unlike other investments like stocks, real estate cannot be easily bought and sold regularly. Therefore, it may not prove to be a suitable investment option for investors seeking short term profits.

Requires Dealing with Market Inefficiencies: Sometimes, the investors who lack the necessary information about the prospective real estate project, pool in their money at not so profitable projects.

No Fixed Maturity: Real estate appraisal does not take place at a fixed rate in a defined period. The capital appreciation in case of properties is a long term process; it is though presumed but not pre-defined.

Reasons for Failure in Real Estate Investing

If not done wisely, real estate investment may even lead to poor returns or depreciation of the investment value.

Following are some of the primary reasons for which the real estate investing goes wrong:

Reasons for Failure in Real Estate Investing

Lack of Knowledge: Before investing in real estate, one must have ample knowledge and information about the project he or she is planning to spend in. Most of the investors fail to analyze the right time of investment or potential of the property and are unable to generate good returns on their sum.

Poor Management: Buying of a suitable property or real estate project as an investment is an art. But the investor needs to equally pay attention towards the management and maintenance of that property, contractors, budget and tenants. In the case of a real estate which is poorly managed, the returns may deplete.

False Calculation: Real estate investing requires a calculative approach and mathematical skills to determine the future profitability of a project. Sometimes, investors lack these particular skills and fund in less beneficial projects.

Giving Up Early: One of the most common mistakes made by an impatient investor is expecting a high return from a real estate investment in a short period. And if it does not happen, they lose hope and give up easily. Such people need to understand that these investments yield high returns in the long run.

Tips for Investing in Real Estate

Investing in real estate is a long term approach and yields high profit in future at a low-risk level. These investment decisions are irreversible.

Therefore, the following tips will help you in making real estate investments even with minimal capital:

Tips for Investing in Real Estate Collaboration or Partnership

If an investor lacks sufficient money for investing in a property which can prove to be a cash cow in future; he or she can convince a friend, family member or any other known person to invest in a partnership.

Use Debts

One may even opt for loans and advances from the bank or other financial institution. Here, the property itself can be kept as collateral, and the interest can be paid from the rent earned.

Location of the Property

People are usually looking for the real estates which are well managed and sounds appealing to them. However, one must focus on the site of the property more, instead of its appearance. An old ugly looking property at a prime location can be availed at a reasonable price and renovated or reconstructed to generate high returns.

* 9 7 9 8 8 4 6 1 6 2 7 8 5 *